Ideas

Jack Ricchiuto

DesigningLife Books

Books by Jack Ricchiuto

Collaborative Creativity / 1996
Accidental Conversations / 2002
Project Zen / 2003
Appreciative Leadership / 2005
Mountain Paths / 2007
Conscious Becoming / 2008
Instructions From The Cook / 2009
The Stories That Connect Us / 2010
The Enchantment Of Casual Origins / 2011
The Joy Of Thriving / 2012
Ordinary Eyes / 2012
The Agile Canvas Field Guide / 2012
Abundant Possibilities / 2013
The Power Of Circles / 2013
Making Sense Of Time / 2014
Beyond Recipes / 2014
Focus / 2015
Smarter Together / 2015
Ideas / 2015

3 | Ideas

Ideas

Published by DesigningLife Books
1020 Kenilworth Avenue
Cleveland OH 44113 USA

ISBN 978-1517281564
Paperback

1. Creativity. Innovation.
I. Title

Printed in the USA

Production: CreateSpace
Cover: Tia Andrako

5 | Ideas

Contents

Ideas

Nutrients

Context

Invitation

I have had the honor to spend the last few decades guiding groups around the world in growing new ideas. They seek dreams their communities never imagined even a generation ago. They seek innovations that disrupt the predictions of spreadsheets. They seek better ways to connect, work, teach, heal, research, build and serve.

Ideas describes 5 idea nutrients that help people grow new ideas together. When people go from stuck to thriving in their collaborative creativity, it's because they have transitioned to the kinds of conversations that have this power.

They discover together how to nurture and shape the growth of ideas into possibilities that work. They learn how to become more supportive than competitive, more curious than right.

They respond to each new idea iteration in ways that germinate, cultivate and mature seed ideas into the abundance of something new that works. They create together what no one can create alone. Their new ideas work because they have grown from the rich soil of diverse perspectives.

Our ability to address the issues of these times and realize the dreams we most cherish will always equal our ability to grow new ideas together. Everything good we do together will occur because we know the ingredients that grow new ideas together.

Jack Ricchiuto
October 2015

Ideas

In the beginning is the idea

Everything we appreciate today started as an idea.

When people experience a more sustainable quality of life, it's because of the myriad things that each began as an idea. Every new advancement in human dignity and rights began as a new idea.

Every story that connects us begins in an idea. We become a vibrant and growing network of people because of our shared stories. The social fabric that builds and joins communities of every kind begins and grows in new ideas.

For those of us who have new ideas regularly in our lives and work, they seem to come out of nowhere. We didn't even have a word for creativity until the

1800s, after eons of human creativity. For many, it is still more mystery and art than science how we intentionally go about realizing and growing new ideas.

Ideas grow in the minds of individuals and the practices of many. Consider how the ideas of phones, cars, cities and economies have grown over the past decades far beyond the ideas of their originators and earliest adoptors.

An idea is a possibility. The more fluent we become in growing ideas, the more we feel we live in an infinite space of possibilities. Everything we call a reality feels like a possibility. When everything appears as an idea, our creativity knows no bounds.

Why we need new ideas

As change remains one of life's prime constants, we are daily greeted with new questions and problems, tensions and conflicts, dreams and opportunities.

Our grandparents in their day could not have even imagined how our world today calls for new ideas. Every call for something better is a call for new ideas. Our capacity for better is equal to our capacity for growing ideas.

Having resources isn't enough. Nothing new is possible if we are resource rich and idea poor. It doesn't matter how much money or power we have. It doesn't matter how many laurels we have to rest on.

Past success has currency in a world of continuity. As soon as change enters into the equation, anything beyond the status quo requires new ideas.

Every new dream requires years of new ideas.

Ideas are living things

We can think of ideas as inert objects. We trade them. We negotiate with them. We judge them as good or bad.

It is more accurate to think of them as living things that can be nurtured and grown. They can also be killed instantly like weeds competing for finite resources and attention. They can be discarded like irrelevant and useless waste. They can be edited and revised. They can urge us into action. They can inspire reflection and research. They can spread and transform.

We are more likely to grow ideas when we think of them as living things, as energy forms, that with a nurturing environment can be grown the way all living things can be grown.

Growth implies change in form and function. In each phase of growth, living things become qualitatively different. They look, feel and act differently than they did in previous phases of being and becoming. This is true for any idea.

Maturation is life emerging in forms that go beyond previous structures. We see this as seeds become flora and embryos become fauna. We see this in living forms of human beings and becomings, in groups and organizations, in communities and networks.

We see this with ideas.

When ideas don't grow

Ideas don't always grow. Like all living things, ideas can fail to grow, survive, thrive and create new significance whenever they encounter hostile environments. The possibilities of failure to thrive are many.

Ideas don't grow when we don't listen to each other. Not listening is judgment. As soon as we say an idea is terrible, irrelevant or great, it doesn't grow. It doesn't matter if the judgement is positive or negative. Either way, ideas fail to grow. They stay in the same form. They don't transform.

One of the more common idea debilitating environments is voting. We divide ideas into acceptable and not acceptable, which translates into worthy and not worthy of more conversation and action.

Entrenched biases are a hostile environment. Biases can be based on an ideology or ism. Every bias declares an idea right or wrong. In both contexts, we loyally support or disloyally reject ideas. They don't grow. They stultify in their existing forms.

Social loyalties can be idea hostile environments. We mindlessly accept the idea of people we feel associated with and reject those of people we feel not associated with.

Our ideas have the best chance of growing in conversations with people who hold their biases lightly, who prefer to stay mindfully curious rather than mindlessly acquiescent or critical.

Tension embraced

Our most fertile opportunities for growing ideas are in tension.

We have no shortage of tension today. Tension is the presence of opposites, differences and conflicts. It's when we feel a sense that we're at odds, when we feel the competition of ideas. We feel there is a right

way, and of course, we are seduced by the notion
our way is right.

As much as we are becoming more globally
connected in all things shared and shareable, we still
live with the vestiges of things that divide us. We still
have the ideas of competing economics, cultures,
religions and politics that are more about division
than connection. We have inherited agendas that
can only be carried out by causing others to fail in
their agendas.

When these conflicts become institutionalized, we
begin believing they are both inevitable and vital to
our survival or thrivancy.

Tension is opportunity for listening, discovery and
new unimagined possibilities. Otherwise, it is

opportunity for argument, killing ideas and doing what is less than what is possible.

When we take an opportunity perspective, tension is no longer a problem to be solved but an possibility to be engaged. So many of our best ideas as humans emerged from tension embraced rather than dreaded or destroyed.

Good ideas

An idea isn't good because we declare it as so. Goodness is not a decision. It's a realization. Reality tells whether an idea is good. An idea is good when it's useful, when it works.

Good ideas are useful in two ways. They spark new variations and possibilities. They serve our purposes and dreams.

As they begin and grow, ideas don't necessarily need to be realistic or perfect. The unrealistic and imperfect can lead to more realistic and perfect in steps, stages and iterations.

Judging an idea as bad diminishes its potential. When we know how to grow ideas, we can start anywhere. Any idea can be a good starting point to grow more useful ideas.

Nutrients

The 5 idea nutrients

Ideas grow in conversations that represent nurturing environments. These feature the 5 idea nutrients of *like, so, and, when* and *else.*

Like provides the warmth from the sun. *So* provides the energy from air. *And* provides the minerals from soil. *When* provides mineral access from water. *Else* provides the soil fertility from microbes.

>**Like**: *What do we like about this idea?*

>**So**: *So can you tell us more about this idea?*

>**And**: *And what could we add to make this idea stronger?*

When: *When could this idea happen, given what needs to come before?*

Else: *How else could we realize the advantages and minimize the disadvantages of this idea?*

Sun: Like

What do we like about this idea?

Every idea has some benefit, some advantage, some upside. We don't have to like all of it. We don't have to agree with it completely. We simply acknowledge its potential value.

When we declare what we like about an idea, people with the idea feel heard. When people feel heard they no longer feel urgency to defend and protect it. They become open to learning about it, from it and beyond it. Ideas grow best when people feel welcome to voice their ideas without self-editing and self-filtering. We are more generative together when we are more relaxed together.

New ideas do not grow when we feel we have to be on the defensive. We put each other on the defensive when our first reaction to any idea is questioning, pushing back, attacking its validity or pointing out its obvious deficiencies and risks. The parts of our brain involved in creativity, passion and clear decision making shut down when we go into judgment mode.

When we say what we like about an idea, we can learn more from and about it. We no longer have to reject or accept it. We allow it to inspire new possibilities.

When we identify anything we like about an idea, what we like gives shape to other possibilities. We build on what we like. Like is the foundation for new differences to consider. We can grow an idea we like in some way. We can start to think of other alternatives and variations.

It's important to be specific. We name all the things we like about an idea and why those matter. We name all likable features, functions and potential benefits and impacts.

Air: So

So can you tell us more about this idea?

Every idea raises questions. We want to know about who, what, when, where, how, why. We want to know if and what about.

Curiosity is the opposite of judgment. It is a space of presence. Ideas grow in the present, not in the past or future.

More questions lead to better questions. There are better questions but we can't judge any question until we see what it leads to. It's just important that we don't reject questions. Each question leads to better questions.

People many times have more in mind than they initially express. The more details we get, the more we can help ideas grow. The more we detail what an idea could be like, the more clearly we become on the potentials of the idea. This is why it's important to ask what else people can tell us about any idea.

Every idea new to us is possibly already happening. This dynamic world is teeming with people who are experimenting with all kinds of things under the radar of our attention. Those of us who spend time daily scanning social and public media are continuously surprised by what we have no idea about.

Biomimicry is a good example. People are finding ways to replace industrially produced products like steel with products naturally occurring in nature that actually perform better at fractions of the production and resource costs.

When we have an idea that we think is new and original, it might not be. It might have already been tried or thought.

When we research an idea, we discover its history. We discover other variations and nuances. Even when it has failed in one context, we realize it has potential merit in ours.

Research provokes new perspectives, questions, angles and views. As we grow ideas, we have more likelihood of growing them as we do research than simply trying to ponder our way into new ideas.

Soil: And

And what could we add to make this idea stronger?

We can add another element, feature or dimension. We can add a twist to it. We can add another way to make it more functional, realistic or feasible in our context.

The addition can be small or large. It can be within or beyond our scope of resources and capabilities.
We think of minimal viable products. What could be the simplest version, given our current resources and capabilities, that could allow us to try it, experiment with it and prototype it.

Both-and is the opposite of either-or. And expands ideas beyond disadvantages.

One way to find new additions is to look into and consider similar functional contexts. If we want new ideas on how to get people shopping locally, we can study how flowers attract insects that help them grow. Every functional analogy will offer a new way of thinking about how to strengthen any idea.

We can use historic contexts where lost traditions could revive new significant possibilities. We can play with writing science fiction in ways that reveal new opportunities possible in the present.

Many new living things have fragile and undeveloped embryonic beginnings. We don't discard them for not popping out mature. We strengthen them along the way to vitality and value.

Water: When

When could this idea happen, given what needs to come before?

In ideas as in life, timing is everything.

Many times the difference between a good idea and a less good idea is timing. An idea is good if it is useful. An idea is useful when its time is right. An idea that appears to be good but is ahead of or behind its time is not useful.

Having a sense of timing gets us considering what else if anything needs to occur for this idea to work. We might discover that we need to put many new things in place in order for a potentially good idea to work.

Asking what would need to happen before this illuminates prerequisites. Many ideas emerge before their time. They are potentially good and we're not ready for them. Other things have to happen first. Knowing what would have to happen first makes any idea more feasible, attractive and possible.

We cannot always know exactly when an idea can become reality. We can make estimates that split the difference between our most optimistic and pessimistic scenarios.

We can identify all the precedent ideas that might need to happen first. The larger and more novel an idea, the more previous steps it will require.

Because an idea can't work today doesn't guarantee it also won't in the future. The idea for a laptop before the typewriter era would have been labelled unworkable, but possible once a typewriter and a thousand other ideas would come to fruition first.

Every big new idea stands on the shoulders of countless previous ideas. It's an interesting exercise to take any innovation today and research or at least consider all the innovations back to the discovery of fire that would have had to happen just to make even one of these an affordable, effective reality today.

Microbes: Else

How else could we realize the advantages and minimize the disadvantages of this idea?

Every idea has downsides. Downsides are costs, issues and problems. They are not necessarily fatal. They are not reasons to abandon the essential goodness of the idea.

They are problems and puzzles to research and solve. They are calls to prototyping alternatives and variations.

Ideas grow best when we name the disadvantages we can see to our own ideas. This opens the space for others to feel free to do the same. This allows us to be realistic together.

The else question is particularly useful when we're at the crossroads of two either-or ideas, such as whether we should give people more freedom or more structure. By definition, polarities of opposites cannot be resolved. The opposing options always exist.

Both sides of polarities have upsides and downsides. The wisest approach is to optimize the upsides of both and minimize the downsides of both. This is the work of identifying how we can make the upsides even more possible and how we can make the downsides even less possible.

We also consider else in the inclusion of other people who can bring new perspectives, questions, alternatives, learning and experience. The more diversity of thinking in a group, the more fertile the ground for growing ideas. When we invite people into growing ideas, we make it clear we're asking them to engage the 5 nutrients in the process.

Fluency

It doesn't matter which nutrient we introduce at any time in the process of growing ideas.

We begin and continue anywhere. We can begin and continue with any kind of like, so, and, when and else.

Order doesn't matter. We can begin with who else should we invite here. We can begin with what else could grow the upsides or decrease the downsides. We can begin with what the research says, and what could strengthen an idea. We can begin with clarifying questions or affirmations of what we immediately like.

Each next evolution can spark the next possibilities. We move one iteration at a time towards greater clarity and coherence. It feels like a beautiful rhythm between divergence and consensus. We seek synergies. We transcend the agendas of self-interest. Trust builds. We move forward at the speed of trust.

Context

Every voice heard

Everyone feels heard because everything voiced gets posted and everything posted gets voiced. No one feels left out. Every single thing is used. As in nature, there is no waste. Everything nurtures something else.

The minimal viable versions of anything bear the benefits of all kinds of emergent details that come about through the chemistries of idea nutrients. Each idea contributes to the next. No idea is conclusive. We get attached to no single idea. We expect every idea to evolve.

No one dominates. No one disappears. We share responsibility for the emergence of the whole because we genuinely feel we are smarter together.

No idea is ultimately more important than those that follow.

Taking ideas personally

Each of us lives along a continuum from less to more experienced in growing ideas.

Many of us have little exposure or explicit learning in the art of growing ideas. We take our ideas personally. We feel liked by people who support and like our ideas and disliked by people who question and dislike our ideas.

When we take ideas personally, we inhibit their growth in defense of their current form. In doing so, we keep ourselves from even seeing new possibilities.

Those of us with more experience don't take our ideas personally. We see their potential as beginnings rather than conclusions. We expect them to have even unseen potential to grow and evolve. We feel a commitment to their growth rather than to their current form.

Even when we voice and invest in them with great confidence or passion, we believe in their capacity to become more and even entirely something else.

We don't expect our first ideas will be our best. Our experience has taught us that more ideas lead to better ideas. Because we know how to grow ideas, we believe in the possibility of their growth.

Growing courage

Courage is commitment to what was once considered not possible.

The list is long of current realities not long ago deemed impossible. Think about the ability of people to have a political voice, to talk to virtually anyone in the world, to get an education in anything on their phone, to choose their work and residence location. Think about the kinds of computing, communication, medical and social technologies unimaginable only a few generations ago.

When we come together in courage, we no longer fear the voices of hopelessness, despair and cynicism. They no longer have power to paralyze us in helplessness. We are no longer victims of uncertainty. We are instead energized by the unknown. We are inspired in our questions.

Every act of violence and victimhood emerges from helplessness. Every urge to have power over others emanates from a deep unreconciled sense of powerlessness. All are expressions of an unembraced courage.

The more fluency we gain in growing ideas, the more courage we have personally and together. The many problems that continue to plague us and dreams that continue to inspire us will only be addressed with courage.

They will not be impacted by fear, caution, pessimism, skepticism or doubt. These are all at root the inability to see the potential of growing ideas in a culture of courage.

Fertile growing media

Growing happens in the synergy of seeds, nutrients and media. We use two core media for the growing of ideas in idea nutrient rich environments: our verbalizations and visualizations.

We make sure everyone voices everything they think. We invite people to respond to any idea with any of the seven idea nutrients. This creates a much more thoughtful and generative rhythm than the superficial staccato of brainstorming.

We make sure everything people think gets verbalized, at the least in posted words. Sketches, pictures and models are rich media for the growing of ideas.

Just visualizing ideas causes them to literally grow before our eyes. Visualization invites collaboration to the point where many of our best ideas grow into forms that are unrecognizable as any one person's or clique's idea.

When we're simply recording ideas in words, it's important that we post only one idea and variation on a card or sticky note. This allows us to see more new connections between ideas, which is far less possible when we constrain ideas to linear lists. This allows us to keep recombining and curating ideas into more useful versions and variations.

The inner game of ideas

Our time growing ideas alone is as important as our time growing ideas together. Our shared capacity for creativity is nourished by personal infusions from reflective time on our own.

We grow ideas on our own using the same 5 idea nutrients. We flow in an improvisational dialogue between ideas that emerge and each nutrient. We shift between just being present, listening, to what comes up and injecting a new ingredient into whatever emerges. This is the inner game of growing new ideas.

It is as important to be sure to visualize at least in words every single thing that emerges and grows.

The simple acts of writing and seeing spark all kinds of unexpected connections.

In every single creative process, what's new is always simply a new way of combining possibilities that already exist. Every invention and innovation is nothing more than unprecedented combinations of existing things.

Making a habit of this kind of creative inner dialogue gives us more mastery in the process, gives us more to share with our creative partners and connects us more deeply to them in our effort together.

The myth of competition

Despite the unsupportable and superstitious folklore about competition being the mother of innovation, competition creates a fear and aggression mindset. We are motivated by fear of failure. Fear shuts down the creativity parts of our brain.

Many innovations come from rogue small teams operating at the edges of competitive mindsets. The reason they are successful in their creativity is because they know how to grow ideas together.

There is no evidence that their commitment to fear and aggression makes new ideas more possible. Innovation and creativity happen not because of competition but in spite of it.

Even the bonds we gain in a common enemy cannot in any way substitute for fluency and shared commitment to the 5 nutrients of growing ideas.

Incentives

As it turns out, incentives reduce capacity for creativity. Teams responsible for the ideas behind our most celebrated innovations worked from a culture of growing ideas in a context of relentless passion for the seeming impossible. They have no sense of certainty even when decorated with more funding and support than they knew what to do with. There were no guarantees for their efforts.

Incentives makes us risk averse. We prematurely give up on potentially promising ideas that suggest anything less than certain success. We go after the security of low hanging fruit instead of growing large trees and orchards of more significant harvests.

The role of leadership

There is no specific role of leadership in growing ideas. People who are formal or informal leaders can be uniquely valuable in introducing the idea nutrients in any conversation.

Fortunately, each nutrient is such a simple question anyone can introduce them anywhere, anytime. It doesn't require having more power, knowledge or responsibility than everyone else. It doesn't require any other literacy than idea nutrient literacy.

Ideas don't grow because we pretend one of us is smarter than all of us. If anything, this intellectual divide reduces the possibilities of emergent and evolving ideas.

When we collude in this pretense, we give more attention and compliance to one person's ideas or the ideas one person approves or endorses. This constrains the free flow of new ideas and nutrients. Potentially good ideas never see the light of day. Ideas die on the vine. Idea seeds go unsown and uncultivated. Growing ideas fail to grow and thrive.

People who have position and power contribute most as peers in the group. When helpful, they can nudge the group into new uses of nutrients to grow the ideas emerging.

Too many ideas

One of the classic ways to protect the status quo is declaring that we already have too many ideas or that if we just let anyone in the conversation, we would have too many ideas.

Each idea is an opportunity for growth. Our world needs so many new ideas. The only way anyone could fear too many ideas is being committed to the status quo.

One of the most generative ways to incubate and grow unlimited ideas is a process invented by Harrison Owen called Open Space.

In the process, we start with a question. It is a big question. It's a question that is new, that people are unprepared for. It is a question that is personal, that matters to people. It is a question that takes us beyond the cliches of easy and old answers. A classic invitation question is: *What kinds of conversations should we be having?*

We ask any sized group gathered in the same local, virtual or blended space what they think we should talk about relative to this question. We ask people who name new conversations to invite others into small groups of two or more focused on the new conversations.

We host as many rounds of new conversations as we have time for. We can engage potentially hundreds of people in days of rounds.

After each round, we ask the whole group what patterns they notice and what the next round of new conversations they would like to invite. The process creates progressive iterations towards spiraling coherence and action. There are never too many ideas. More ideas lead to better ideas. More conversations lead to better conversations.

The process realizes velocity, meaning and agility to the extent that people grow ideas in a media of the 5 rich idea nutrients.

People are free to stay in single conversations where they feel they can contribute or learn the most or move between multiple conversations. People who move between conversations spread ideas and create new connections and alignments.

Rethinking wealth

New ideas are the new wealth. Lives, communities and businesses are transforming because of the currencies of new ideas.

With unprecedented expanses of connectivity, the planet is in a deep transition. There is no possible way we can sustainably, sensibly or intelligently live in this connection era as we did in previous eras. Among the many ways we're rethinking how we live, we're rethinking wealth.

In eras where disconnection was accepted as fact of life, ultimate wealth was economic. Economic wealth works for the advantaged because it sustains the status quo that benefits them. It keeps divided people divided.

In this era of connection, we're talking more about the wealth of new ideas. New ideas connect people. Unlike financial capital and status, new ideas are capable of being distributed, shared and a source of boundaryless empowerment.

Since the original ideas of domesticated fire and water vessels, new ideas have disrupted the economic status quo. That is their nature. Every time we grow new ideas together, we are making possible new kinds of wealth that transcend the singularly economic.

We create new kinds of social, cultural, spiritual, intellectual and artistic wealth that leverages the power of connections in ways previous generations and eras could not even imagine.

A vision for idea fluency

Growing ideas is a pattern language. With learning and mastery, we can grow fluency in the language of ideas.

The more idea fluency we invite and practice in every dimension of personal, work and community life, the more possible it will be to dream large and realize our dreams.

Breaking through the status quo takes new ideas that work. Even when a new idea wows us, it still takes a diligent process of growing it into what works. Each new use context challenges an idea to iterate in new adaptations and disruptive alternatives.

Idea fluency can begin, and does begin, at any early age. The vast majority young children practice idea fluency. This fluency decreases to a small minority through their life span. This is ironic given the science indicating that our brain's capacity for creativity increases with age because we have more dots to connect and get better at pattern consciousness.

All we have to do is invite it and introduce people to any or all of the 5 idea nutrients so they can grow mastery in idea fluency.

In an idea fluent world, we will see more people thrive. We will see people come alive in a more beautiful world they shape together.

65 | Ideas

Jack Ricchiuto

Jack is a writer who teaches teams and leaders how to be smarter together. He is the originator of the Agile Canvas model that is revolutionizing the way we organize for organizational thrivancy.

As a 19-time author, Jack has been delivering workshops and coaching over the past 3 decades, in over 24 industry sectors with hundreds of organizations and dozens of communities across the US and globally. Jack's work is based on his experience, his writing and the latest science and research.

Jack has worked with multi-national companies, foundations and non-profits like IBM, PayPal, NASA, American Red Cross, Nestle, FedEx, Federal Reserve Bank, USDA, Switzer Foundation, E&Y, Smucker and investment leaders from Silicon Valley. He is a managing partner with Thrive@Work and Medato.

He has taught in graduate and post-graduate programs in the areas of storytelling, leadership, community building and career development including at Harvard Kennedy Business School, UC Berkeley, Vanderbilt, Tecnologico de Monterrey and Leadership for 15 years in Kent State University's EMBA program. He was one of the first web site designers, bloggers and social media and network experts.

Jack's 19 books include *Collaborative Creativity, Accidental Conversations, Project Zen, Appreciative Leadership, Mountain Paths, Conscious Becoming, Instructions from the Cook, The Stories that Connect Us, The Enchantment of Casual Origins, The Joy of Thriving, Ordinary Eyes, The Agile Canvas Field Guide, Abundant*

Possibilities, The Power Of Circles, Making Sense Of Time, Beyond Recipes, Focus, Smarter Together and *Ideas.*

With a graduate degree in positive psychology from Goddard College, Jack was trained by global leaders in American, European and Japanese therapeutic transformation models. Jack continues to coach entrepreneurs and intrapreneurs as he has since the late 90s.

Visit <u>JackRicchiuto.com</u>

71 | Ideas